Think of the Possibilities

by Susan Ostrowski
illustrated by Julie Olson

HOUGHTON MIFFLIN   BOSTON

Printed in China

ISBN 10: 0-618-90033-0
ISBN 13: 978-0-618-90033-6

23456789 NOR 16 15 14 13 12 11 10 09 08

Kamala, Lian, and Rodrigo walked home from school together each day. Today they had permission to stop at a special place: the new sundae shop. When the final bell rang, the three friends met in front of the school.

"I've been looking forward to this all day," Kamala said, taking Lian by the arm and walking down the sidewalk. Ten minutes later, the friends were inside Martin's Sundae Shop. Mr. Martin, the owner, greeted them.

"Here is how it works, kids: you create your own sundae," he said. "You choose the ice cream, the topping, and the extras you want. Then I make the sundae for you."

"What are our options?" asked Kamala.

"You can have chocolate, vanilla, or strawberry ice cream," said Mr. Martin, pointing to the ice cream in the cooler. "The toppings are fudge, caramel, and marshmallow. They're here on the counter. Then you can finish off the sundae with the extras, which are nuts, sprinkles, or coconut."

"Wow, we can make a lot of different sundaes!" said Rodrigo.

"Absolutely," smiled Mr. Martin. "Let me know when you decide what you want."

Read·Think·Write If Mr. Martin had only two kinds of ice cream and two kinds of toppings, how many different sundae combinations could he make?

Lian turned to Kamala. "I have no idea what kind I want!"

"Me neither, but I think it might be easier to decide if we knew what all the possible sundae combinations are," suggested Kamala.

"That's a great idea!" said Lian. "Let's name them all. We can have chocolate ice cream with caramel topping and sprinkles, or vanilla with fudge topping and nuts." Kamala and Rodrigo joined in, naming other combinations. After a few minutes, Rodrigo said, "Hold on. We already said vanilla with caramel and coconut."

"This isn't working," Kamala said. "I think we need to make an organized list so we can keep track of all the possible combinations and not repeat any."

"Okay." Rodrigo took a notebook and pen from his backpack. "Let's start listing all the possible sundaes we can make with chocolate ice cream. I'll write them."

"There's chocolate with fudge and nuts," said Kamala.

"And chocolate with fudge and sprinkles," offered Lian.

"Then chocolate with fudge and coconut," said Rodrigo, writing the list.

"Now chocolate with caramel, so it would be chocolate, caramel, and nuts," said Kamala.

"Yes, then chocolate, caramel, and sprinkles," added Lian.

"And chocolate, caramel, and coconut," finished Kamala.

Read·Think·Write What have the friends done to make their list organized?

5

The friends continued to list combinations. "Did we do strawberry with fudge yet?" asked Kamala.

"No," said Lian. "There's strawberry–fudge–nuts, strawberry–fudge–sprinkles, and strawberry–fudge–coconut."

"That's it, then," announced Rodrigo.

"No, we forgot strawberry with marshmallow topping," said Kamala.

"So there's strawberry–marshmallow–nuts, strawberry–marshmallow–sprinkles, and strawberry–marshmallow–coconut," said Rodrigo as he wrote.

"Well, did we list all the possibilities?" asked Lian as the friends reviewed the organized list.

"I think so," said Rodrigo. "I count 27 combinations. And I know which one I'll be eating!"

"Me, too," smiled Kamala, as Lian nodded her head.

"How are you kids doing?" asked Mr. Martin, walking up to their table.

"We just made a list of all the possible sundae combinations here," said Lian as Mr. Martin studied the list.

"I should put up a sign like this so customers can see all the sundaes they can make," said Mr. Martin.

"You can have our list," offered Rodrigo.

"Well, thanks! And because of your good idea, your sundaes are free today," said Mr. Martin.

The friends cheered and wasted no time telling Mr. Martin what sundaes they wanted.

Read•Think•Write If Mr. Martin served three kinds of ice cream, three kinds of toppings, and only two kinds of extras, how many possible sundae combinations could he make?

Responding

1. Marietta has brown pants, green pants, and black pants. She has a red shirt and a green shirt. What are all the different pant–shirt combinations she can make?

2. Tim is making a sandwich. He can use either cheese, turkey, salami, or bologna. He can spread on either mayonnaise, ketchup, or mustard. How many different kinds of sandwiches can Tim make using one meat or cheese and one condiment?

3. **Recognize Main Idea** Once a week, Mrs. Wells pairs up sixth-graders with second-graders and has them read to each other. This week, the sixth-graders are Mara, Brian, Kianna, and Larry. The second-graders are Kelvin, Hiro, Cliff, and Pedro. How many different sixth-grade–second-grade pairings can Mrs. Wells make?

Activity

With two partners, use a number cube and a spinner that has different colors. Find all the possible number–color combinations.